52 (MORE) FLOWER MANDALAS

AN ADULT COLORING BOOK FOR INSPIRATION AND STRESS RELIEF

BY DAVID J. BOOKBINDER AND MARY O'MALLEY

TRANSFORMATIONS PRESS

52 (more) Flower Mandalas: An Adult Coloring Book for Inspiration and Stress Relief

ISBN: 978-0-9846994-2-1

Mail:	David J. Bookbinder
	Transformations Press
	85 Constitution Lane
	Danvers, MA 01923
Email:	transformations@davidbookbinder.com
Phone:	978-395-1292
Websites:	davidbookbinder.com/books
	maryomalleyart.com
	flowermandalas.org
Social media:	facebook.com/groups/52flowermandalas

Printed in the United States of America.

INTRODUCTION

The literal meaning of the word *mandala* is "circle." Mandalas appear in natural phenomena such as flowers and galaxies, and people have been creating them throughout human history. Mandalas signify wholeness. They can represent unity on a cosmic scale, and they are also tools for finding the unity in ourselves. Carl Jung, one of the founders of modern psychotherapy, saw mandalas as a pathway to the essential Self.

52 (more) Flower Mandalas: An Adult Coloring Book for Inspiration and Stress Relief was a collaboration. The mandalas in this book began as flower photographs I took in neighborhoods, shops, botanical gardens, and the homes of friends and family. From these flower photos I created Flower Mandalas, blending photography with digital art. You can see a collection of these images at flowermandalas.org.

The 52 exquisite Flower Mandala coloring pages in this book were drawn by artist Mary O'Malley. Mary has transformed the Flower Mandala images into a family of illustrations that invite you to create your own unique works of art. You can see more of Mary's art at maryomalleyart.com.

Mary and I invite you to continue the collaboration. Check out what other colorists are doing and post your Flower Mandala creations on the Amazon.com book page, the 52 Flower Mandalas Facebook group (52 Flower Mandalas), or the colorist gallery (davidbookbinder.com/books/gallery). And please let us know what you'd like to see in a sequel.

There are many reasons to color. Some do it to relax. Some to enter a different mental/emotional/spiritual space, and others as a kind of self-therapy. But coloring is also just plain fun! So — in the immortal words of author Maurice Sendak, who spoke to the child in all of us — let the wild rumpus start!

— David J. Bookbinder and Mary O'Malley

ABOUT DAVID J. BOOKBINDER

David J. Bookbinder is a writer, photographer, and psychotherapist. His award-winning Flower Mandala images were inspired by the paintings of Georgia O'Keeffe and the flower photographs of Harold Feinstein, with whom he briefly studied. David has been taking photographs since he was six. He came to psychotherapy after a transformative near-death experience shifted him toward art and healing. David holds Masters degrees in Counseling Psychology and Creative Writing. His other books include *Paths to Wholeness: Fifty-Two Flower Mandalas*, *52 Flower Mandalas: An Adult Coloring Book for Inspiration and Stress Relief*, as well as a book on American folk music and three books on computer software.

ABOUT MARY O'MALLEY

Mary O'Malley is an artist and illustrator whose primary medium is drawing. Inspired by forms and patterns in nature, her work is characterized by intricate detail and a labor-intensive process that becomes a meditative experience for both artist and viewer. Mary earned her Bachelor of Fine Arts from the Massachusetts College of Art and Design in 1997; in 2005 she received her Master of Fine Arts from the School of Visual Arts in New York. Her work has been exhibited widely, and she has been the recipient of several grants. She lives and works on the New Hampshire Seacoast.

In the right light, at the right time, everything is extraordinary.

\- Aaron Rose

First there is a mountain, then there is no mountain,
then there is.

- Donovan

Creativity requires the courage to let go of certainties.

- Erich Fromm

Nothing is softer or more flexible than water, yet nothing can resist it.

- Lao Tzu

Go confidently in the direction of your dreams. Live the life you've imagined.

- Henry David Thoreau

Trust yourself. You know more than you think you do.

— Benjamin Spock

The only thing constant in life is change.

- François de la Rochefoucauld

Whatever you do will be insignificant, but it is very important that you do it.

- Mohandas Gandhi

However long the night, the dawn will break.

- African Proverb

There is no cure for birth and death save to enjoy the interval.

- George Santayana

Don't look for miracles. You yourself are the miracle.

- Henry Miller

Logic will get you from A to B. Imagination will take you everywhere.

- Albert Einstein

A kiss is a lovely trick, designed by nature, to stop words when speech becomes superfluous.

- Ingrid Bergmen

You must do the thing you think you cannot do.

\- Eleanor Roosevelt

If you don't blow your own horn, nobody else will.

- Jimmy Breslin

The pain passes, but the beauty remains.

- Pierre Auguste Renoir

Where there is hatred let me sow love.

- Saint Francis of Assisi

You play. You win. You play. You lose. You play.

- Jeanette Winterson

May you live every day of your life.

- Jonathan Swift

The cure for boredom is curiosity. There is no cure for curiosity.

- Dorothy Parker

Against the assault of laughter nothing can stand.

- Mark Twain

Sometimes the heart sees what is invisible to the eye.

- H. Jackson Brown Jr.

Just living is not enough. One must have sunshine, freedom, and a little flower.

\- Hans Christian Andersen

Always be a little kinder than necessary.

\- James M. Barrie

God, grant me the serenity to accept the things I cannot change,
Courage to change the things I can,
And wisdom to know the difference.

- Reinhold Niebuhr

Nothing is particularly hard if you divide it into small jobs.

- Henry Ford

When it is dark enough, you can see the stars.

- Ralph Waldo Emerson

What the caterpillar calls the end, the rest of the world calls a butterfly.

- Lao Tzu

The only real voyage of discovery consists not in seeking new landscapes but in having new eyes.

- Marcel Proust

Different strokes for different folks.

\- Sly & the Family Stone

Find something you're passionate about and keep tremendously interested in it.

- Julia Child

Never doubt that a small group of thoughtful, committed citizens can change the world. Indeed, it is the only thing that ever has.

- Margaret Mead

A moment's insight is sometimes worth a life's experience.

- Oliver Wendell Holmes

We are just an advanced breed of monkeys on a minor planet of a very average star, but we can understand the Universe. That makes us something very special.

- Stephen Hawking

Without warning
as a whirlwind
swoops on an oak
Love shakes my heart.

– Sappho

Only put off until tomorrow what you are willing to die having left undone.

- Pablo Picasso

There's a bit of magic in everything, and some loss to even things out.

- Lou Reed

I wonder if anyone notices
I'm using the company car
on company time
to research a single flower?

— Wallace Stevens

When you change the way you look at things, the things you look at change.

\- Wayne Dyer

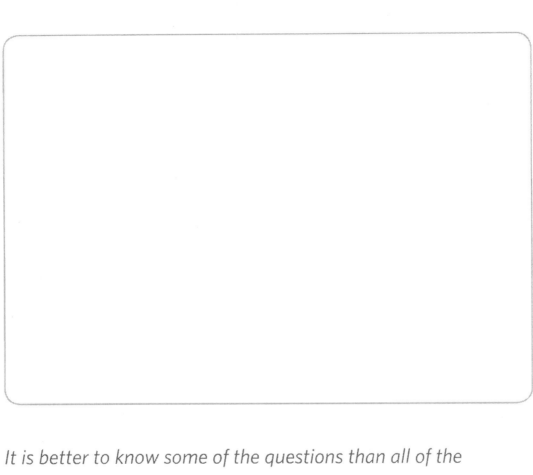

It is better to know some of the questions than all of the answers.

- James Thurber

Don't let the noise of others' opinions drown out your own inner voice.

- Steve Jobs

At any moment you have a choice that either leads you closer to your spirit or further away from it.

- Thich Nhat Hanh

We are continually faced with a series of great opportunities brilliantly disguised as insoluble problems.

- John W. Gardner

Happiness is like a butterfly which, when pursued, is always beyond our grasp, but, if you will sit down quietly, may alight upon you.

- Nathaniel Hawthorne

If not you, who? If not now, when?

- Rabbi Hillel

Gratitude unlocks the fullness of life. It turns what we have into enough, and more.

- Melody Beattie

Chase down your passion like it's the last bus of the night.

- Terri Guillemets

Real generosity toward the future lies in giving all to the present.

- Albert Camus

Only those who will risk going too far can possibly find out how far one can go.

- T.S. Eliot

This phantasm
of falling petals vanishes into
moon and flowers.

- Okyo

Great things do not just happen by impulse, but are a succession of small things linked together.

- Vincent Van Gogh

I am not discouraged, because every wrong attempt discarded is another step forward.

- Thomas Edison

37062663R00063

Made in the USA
Middletown, DE
18 November 2016